Bobby, Tabitha, Josh and Waldo are on the train.

They are happy.

Pearson Education Limited
Edinburgh Gate, Harlow,
Essex CM20 2JE, England
and Associated Companies throughout the world.

ISBN: 978-1-4479-7995-1

This edition first published by Pearson Education Ltd 2014

10

Text copyright © Pearson Education Ltd 2014

Set in 19/23pt OT Fiendstar Semibold
Printed in Slovakia by Neografia

Illustrations: Adam Clay

For a complete list of the titles available in the Pearson English Kids Readers series, please go to
www.pearsonenglishkidsreaders.com. Alternatively, write to your local Pearson Education office or to
Pearson English Readers Marketing Department, Pearson Education, Edinburgh Gate, Harlow, Essex CM202JE, England.

Activity page

Before You Read

1 Match the words and pictures.

1 balloon ☐
2 train ☐
3 elephant ☐
4 fair ☐
5 chocolate ☐

ⓐ ⓑ ⓒ ⓓ ⓔ

After You Read

1 Find these pictures in the story. What color are they?

blue   **brown**   orange   **red**   yellow

ⓐ ⓑ ⓒ ⓓ ⓔ

2 Match the characters to the pictures, then say.

Tabitha   Josh   Bobby   Waldo

Tabitha has a book.

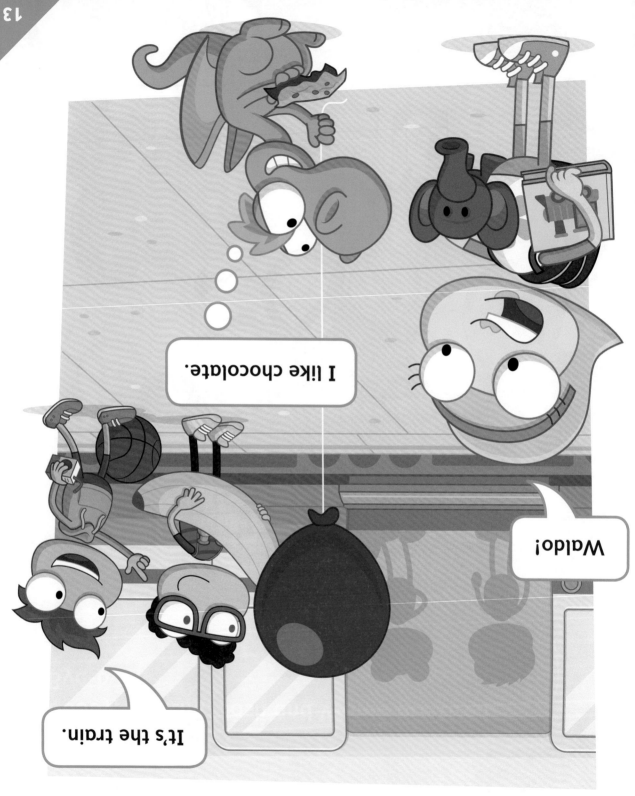

The elephant is in the water.

Tabitha is happy.
Waldo is not happy.